ABOUT VAHRAM MURATYAN

His debut illustrated book
was an international bestseller in 2012.
The simple lines, bright block colors,
and witty words of *Paris versus New York*
ushered readers into a playful and surprising world,
and have earned Vahram collaborations
with prestigious luxury brands.
Vahram also contributes a weekly illustration to *M*,
the weekend magazine supplement of *Le Monde*,
where he spices up an elegant take on Parisian culture
with a touch of irony and affectionate eccentricity.
Vahram Muratyan divides his time
between Paris and New York.
And his work takes him all over the world.

www.vahrammuratyan.com

ABOUT TIME

Also by Vahram Muratyan

Paris
versus
New York
A TALLY OF TWO CITIES

VAHRAM MURATYAN

ABOUT TIME

A VISUAL MEMOIR AROUND THE CLOCK

LITTLE, BROWN AND COMPANY
New York | Boston | London

Little, Brown and Company
Hachette Book Group
1290 Avenue of the Americas, New York, NY 10104
littlebrown.com

First Edition: November 2014

Little, Brown and Company is a division of Hachette Book Group, Inc. The Little, Brown name
and logo are trademarks of Hachette Book Group, Inc.

The publisher is not responsible for websites (or their content) that are not owned by the publisher.

The Hachette Speakers Bureau provides a wide range of authors for speaking events.

To find out more, go to hachettespeakersbureau.com or call (866) 376-6591.

ISBN 978-0-316-411004
Library of Congress Control Number: 2014940684

10 9 8 7 6 5 4 3 2 1

IM

Printed in China

*Dedicated to the best storytellers,
my grandparents Zabel and Arman, Mari and Aram*

packing check-in security   customs duty-free

DEPARTURE

take-off

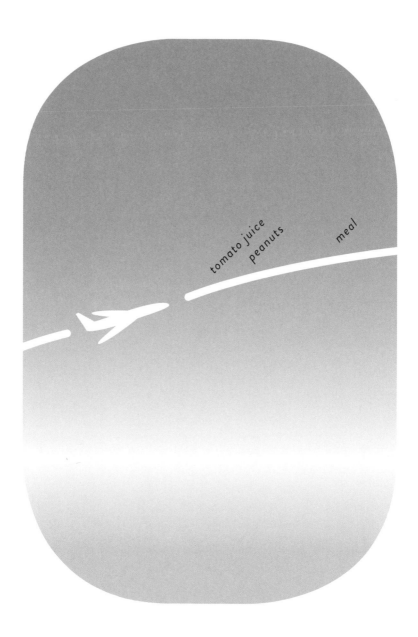

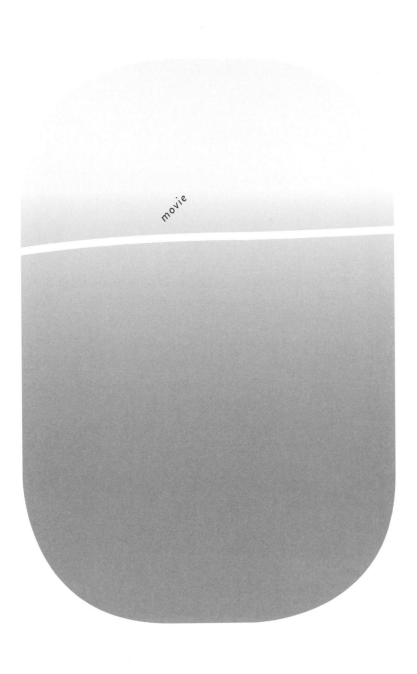

movie

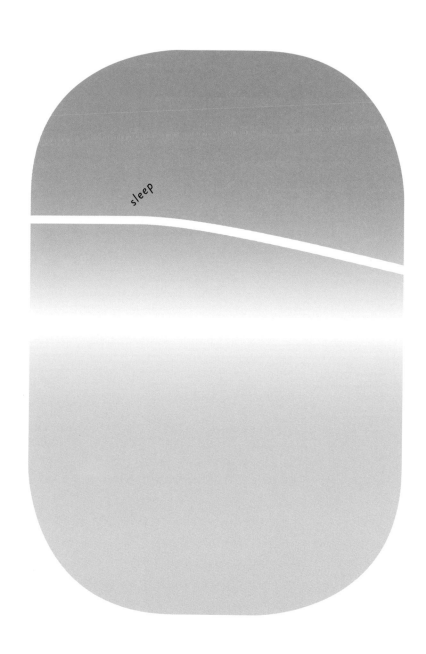

sleep

turbulence

bathroom

prepare for landing

Everything around us is accelerating, time flies
like never before, and experiences bombard us
from all directions — from screens and through phone
lines, in person and in email, across continents
or the dinner table. We live in an age when so much
is spread out before us, when we want it all and
certainly too much. Time defines our relationships,
our memories, our dreams and hopes. Looking
backward, everything is calmer, gentler, simpler.
Time and distance filter, polish or erase certain
moments. Only our wildest passions, laughter
and most painful wounds persist.

'ALL YOU NEED IS TIME

Today, information is king: our world is super-
connected. Everything seems available and yet much
is beyond reach, and nothing is built to last.
Time is capricious. Time changes her mood:
sometimes stingy, often greedy.
If we ask too much, she could swallow us whole.

So it's about time. Slow down.
Press pause.
Look closer, look deeply and imagine
what you might do with your time.

TOO LONG

get in line

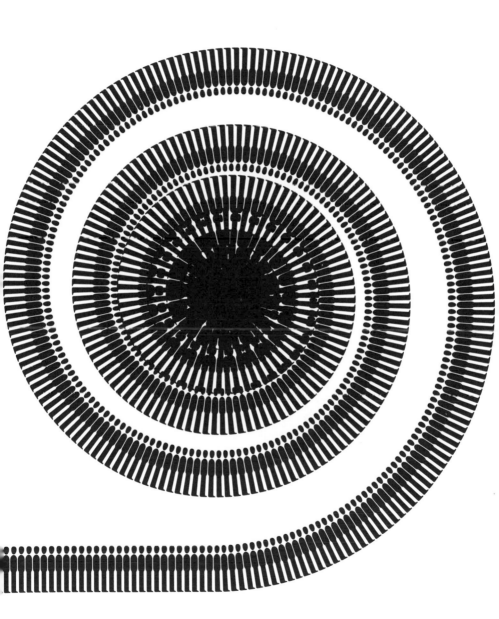

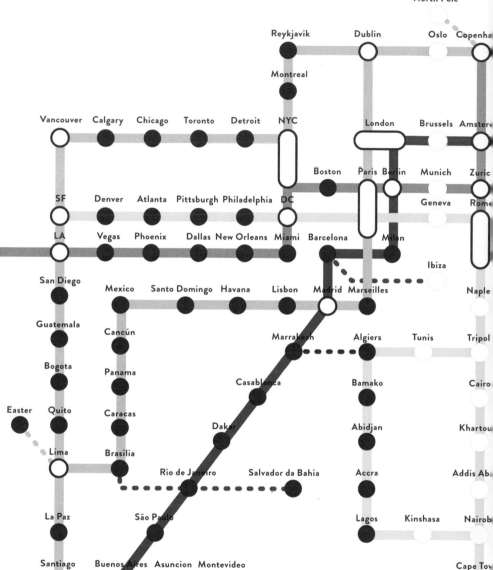

SHORT CUTS

so far yet so close

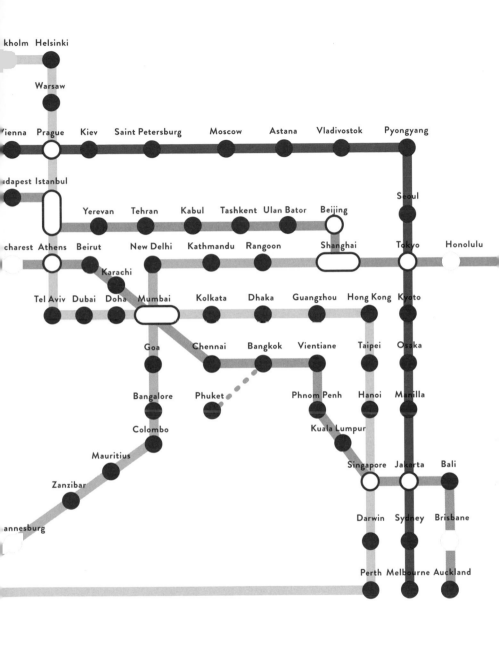

ONE
love at first sight
SECOND

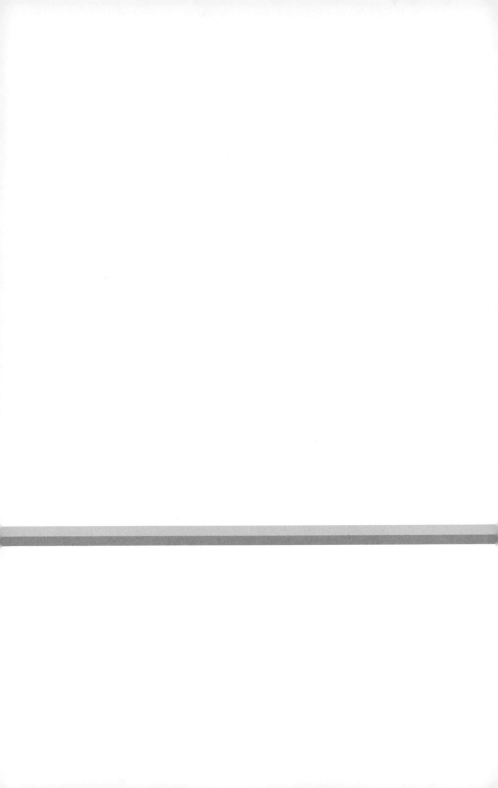

ONE FINE DAY

for all the days of my life

 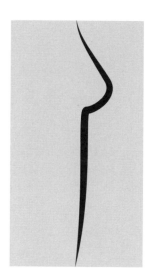 

NiNE MONTHS

a work in progress

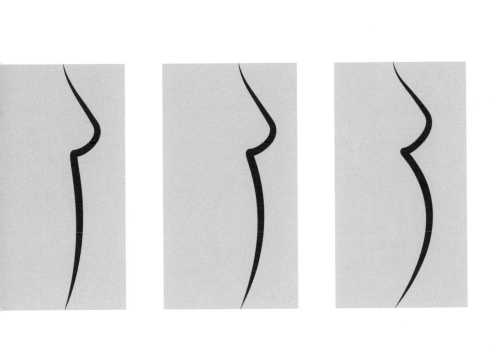

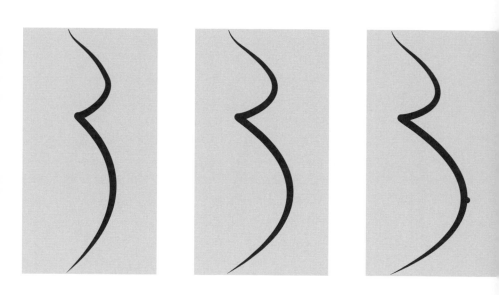

FIRST
the beginning
DAY

1900

1920

visionary great-grandfather
eccentric great-grandmother
boring great-uncle
clever great-aunt
brave grandfather
foodie grandmother
self-made uncle
elegant aunt
quiet father
protective mother
funny cousin
smart brother
cheeky sister

1940

1960

PAST
PERFECT

the sum of them all

1980

2000

2020

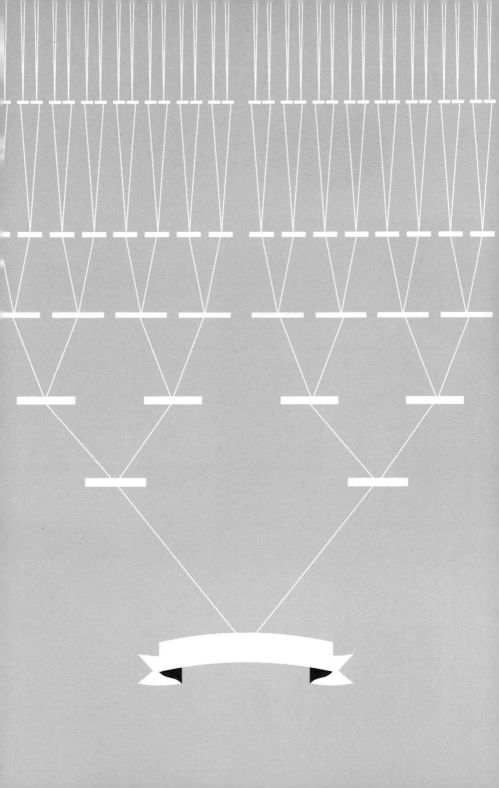

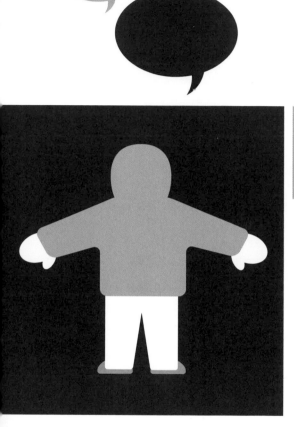

LEARNING CURVE *getting the hang of it*

searching

not found

keep looking

WASTED *HOURS*

everything's upside down

still unfound

stop looking

buy another one

found

1 year old

5 years old

ACQUIRED TASTE

water is overrated

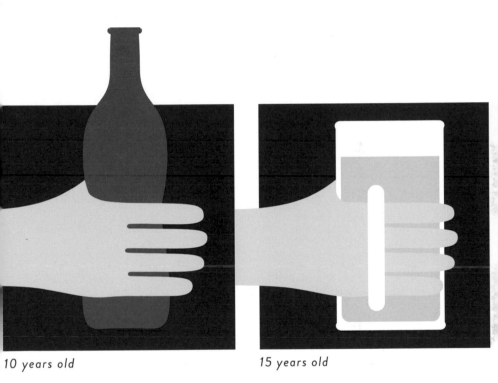

10 years old   15 years old

TIME WILL TELL

all about lies

watch out for the tooth fairy

Santa's coming

he's not dead, just sleeping

believing in prince charming

the perfect woman exists

have your people call my people

TEN YEARS APART

girls grow wild

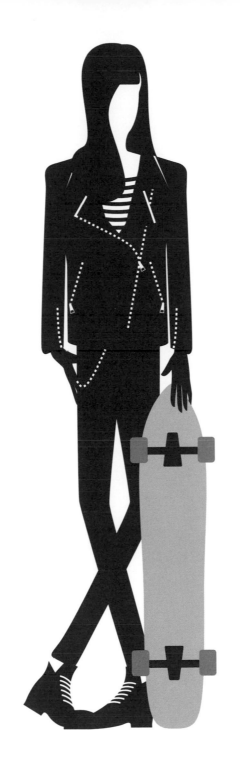

*S*HELF LIFE

years

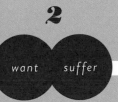

2 3 4 5

THE SURPRISE

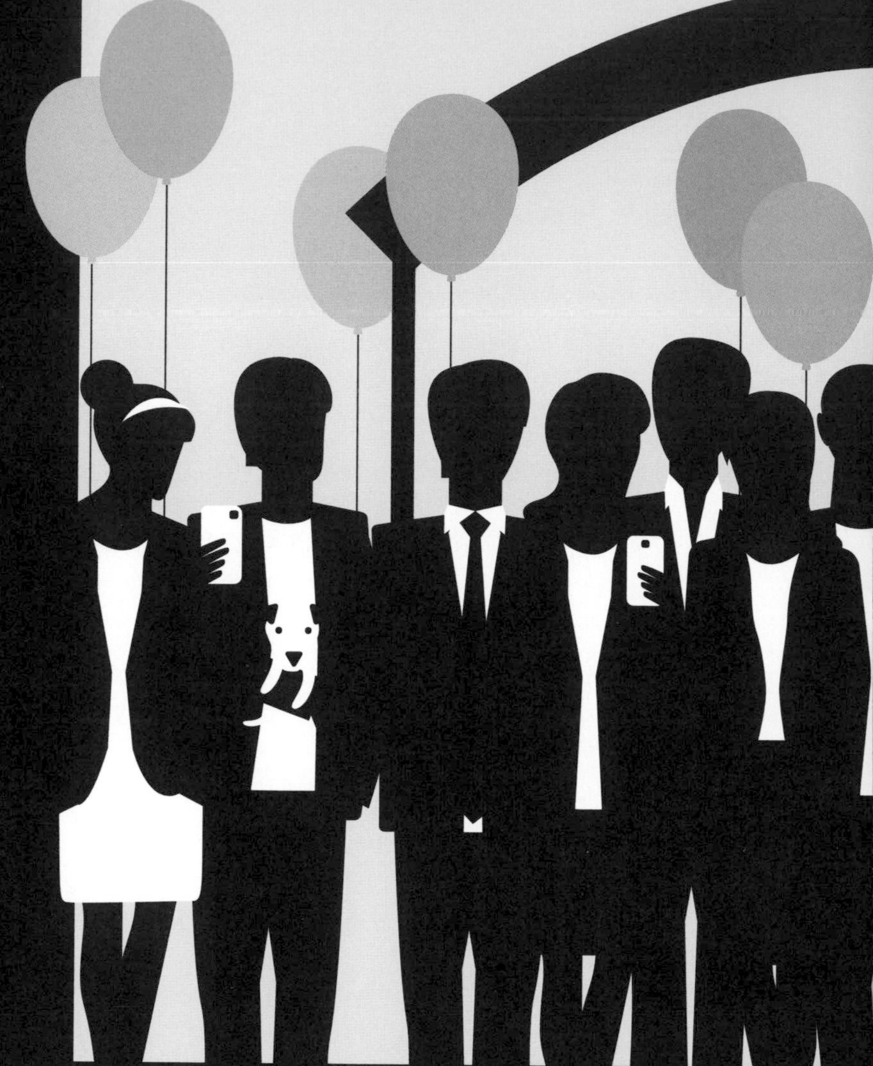

THE MOMENT BEFORE

admit it, you hated it

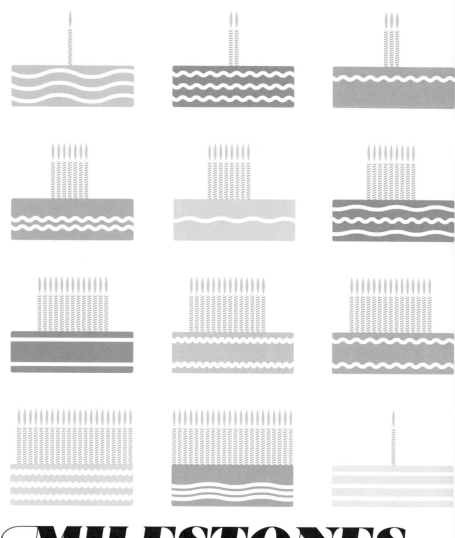

MILESTONES

wish no one was counting anymore

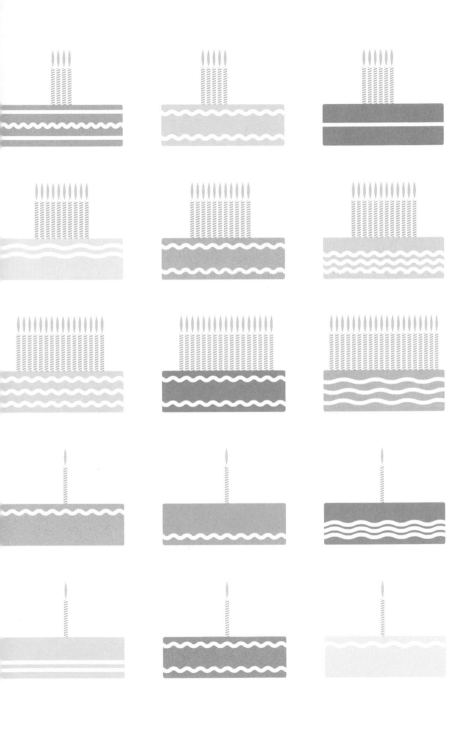

THE OLD

WHEN I WAS YOUNG

I wanted to grow up fast

GETTING
just give time time
THROUGH

RHYTHM & BLUES

life's a bitch...
and a beauty

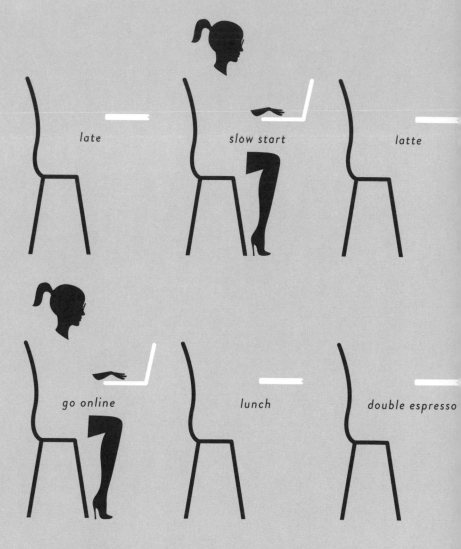

email

meeting

another email

hurry

last minute

yoga

DAILY GRIND

every task you undertake

becomes a piece of cake

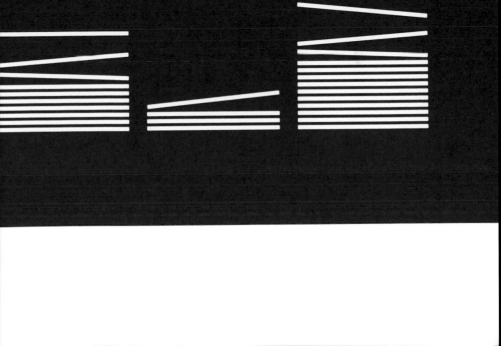

BREATHE

CAN'T HURRY LOVE

it's a game of give and take

SPEED DATING

one chance at a first impression

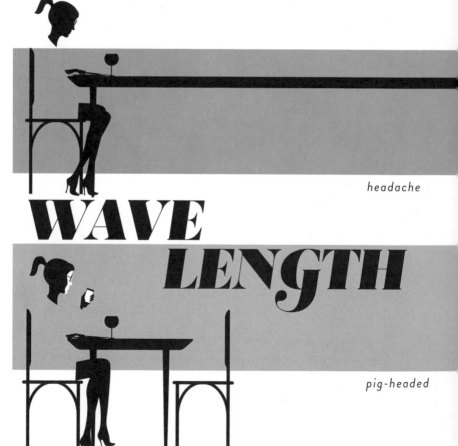

head over heels

WAVE LENGTH

headache

pig-headed

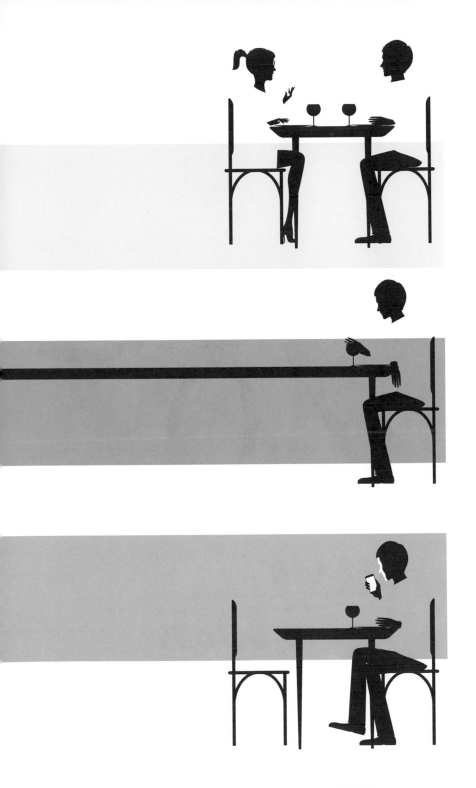

FIRST, *not the last* TIME

disagree

agree

TIME
BOMB *love hurts*

break up

make up

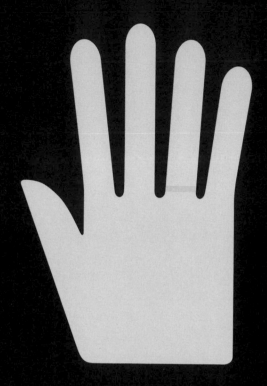

THE SEVEN YEAR ITCH

committed

cheating

abstinence

divorce

all that's fit to print and more

CHECK AGAIN

hair-trigger response

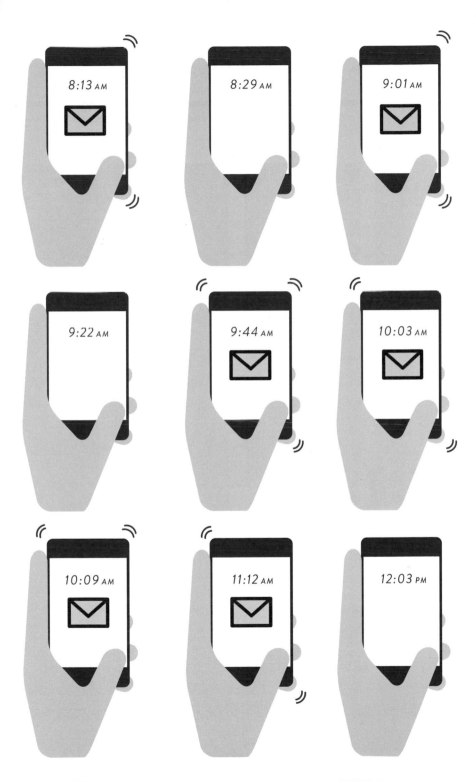

sunday

running

news

brunch

BURN OUT

nap

movies

monday

breakfast

swimming pool

lunch

coffee

binge-watching

tuesday

lie in

stretching

book club

tennis

happy hour

concert

wednesday

pilates

farmers market

matinee

food shopping

cooking class

restaurant

ursday	friday	saturday	sunday
ndon calling	english breakfast	news	lie in
	walk in hyde park	trip to the coast	brunch
	museum tour		opera
ht lunch		lunch	
opping			
	one-man show	casino	
b			sushi evening
usical	burger place	nightswimming	
nner			rest
	cocktail club		

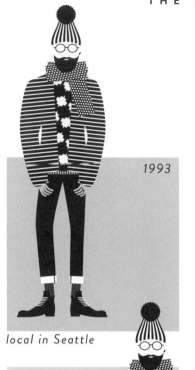

1993

local in Seattle

2004

student in Tokyo

1984

flu in Rio

2008

hip in New York

ENDLESS COMEBACK

everything's relative

1972

dandy in Paris

2010

artist in Berlin

2014

expat in Dubai

1988

casual in London

A LIQUID LIFE

candy is dandy but liquor is quicker

STUCK IN A RUT

won't grow up

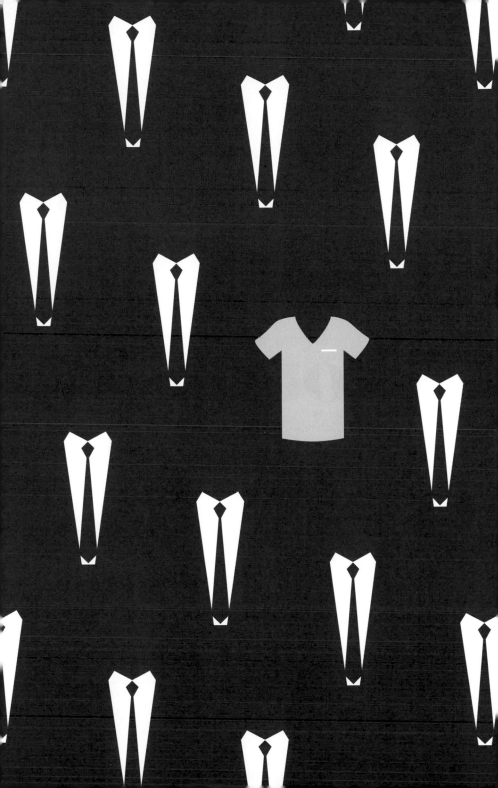

AROUND THE CLOCK

warm up, work out, cool down

FUTURE PERFECT

*steady gig or risky business:
place your bets*

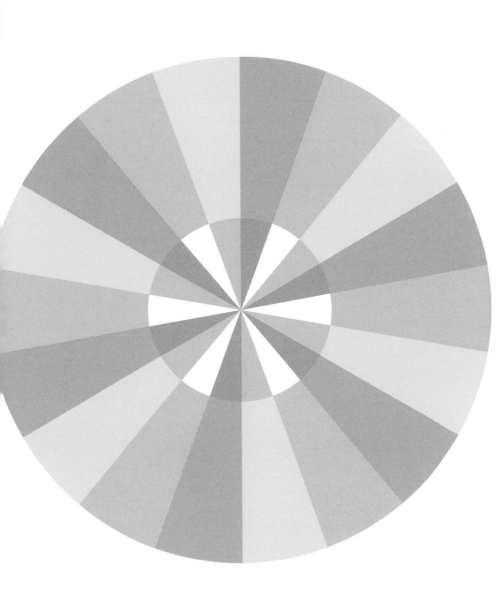

JUDGEMENT DAY

to be or not to be

the **SHORTER** *the* **BETTER**

TIPPING POINT

from mind to mainstream

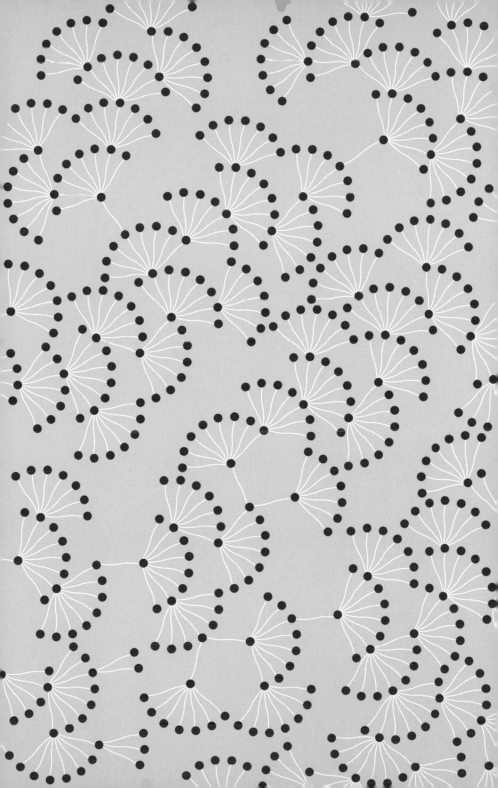

6 AM

9 AM

RUSH
HOUR

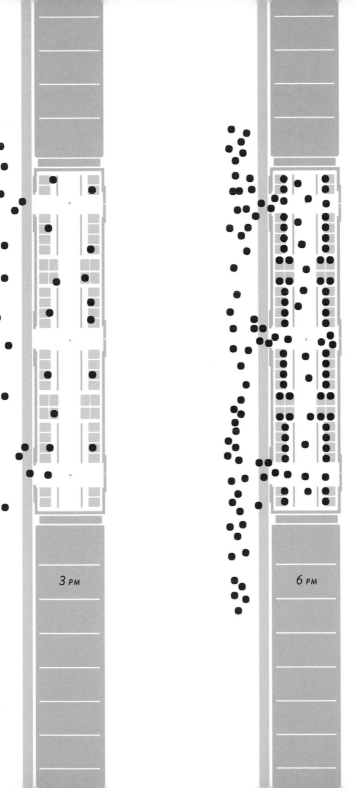

3 PM

6 PM

TIME STANDS STILL

mind the gap

SATURDAY SHOPPING

highway to hell

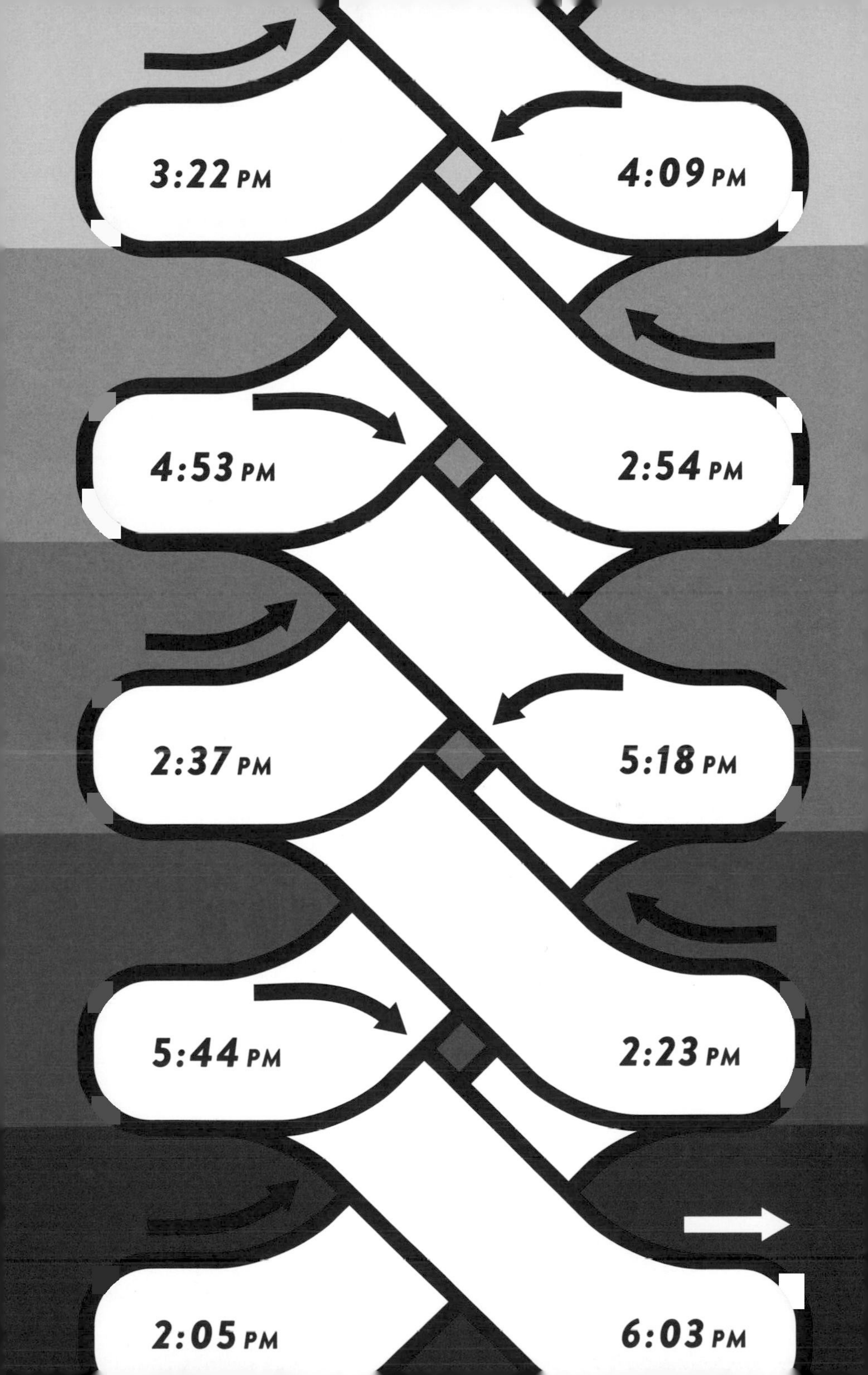
3:22 PM
4:09 PM
4:53 PM
2:54 PM
2:37 PM
5:18 PM
5:44 PM
2:23 PM
2:05 PM
6:03 PM

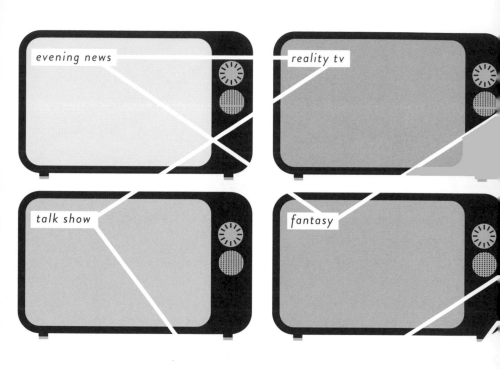

evening news

reality tv

talk show

fantasy

SUNDAY NIGHT

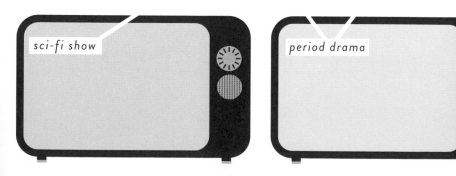

sci-fi show

period drama

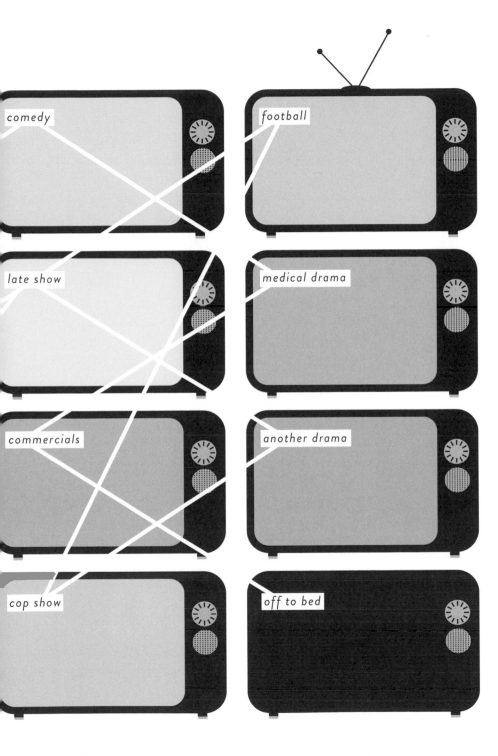

90 MINUTES

one half-time plus extra time

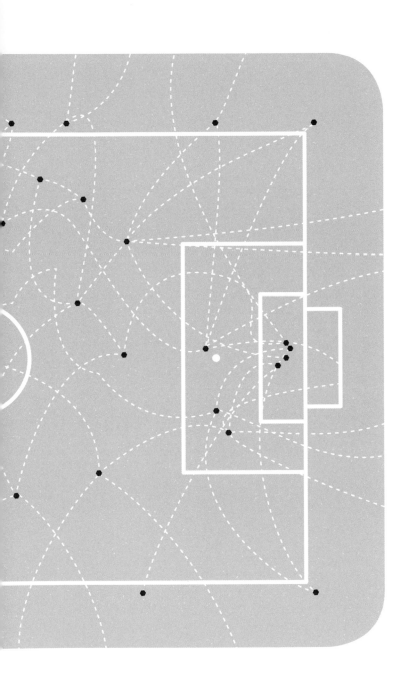

SHOW TIME
the seconds before, the moment after

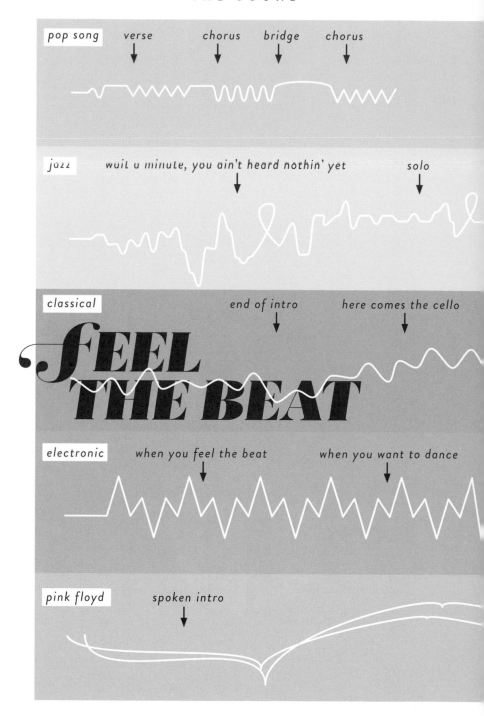

pop song

verse   chorus   bridge   chorus

jazz

wait a minute, you ain't heard nothin' yet   solo

classical

end of intro   here comes the cello

FEEL THE BEAT

electronic

when you feel the beat   when you want to dance

pink floyd

spoken intro

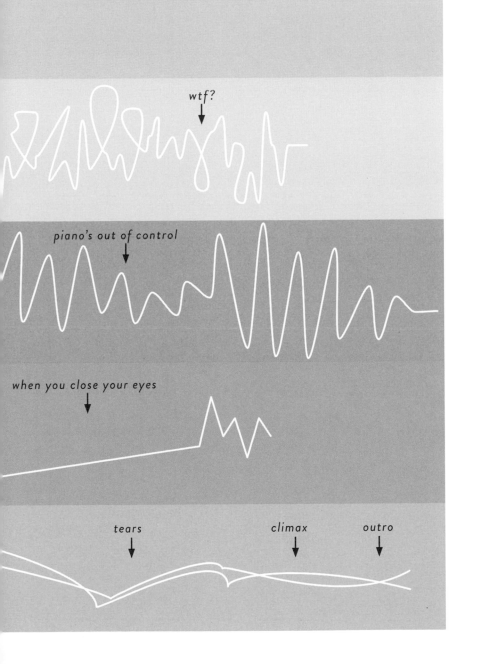

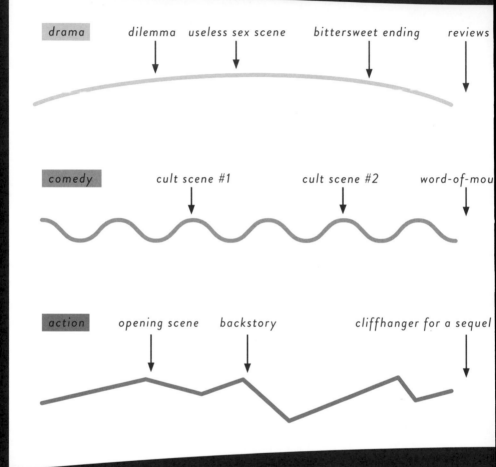

drama

dilemma   useless sex scene   bittersweet ending   reviews

comedy

cult scene #1   cult scene #2   word-of-mou

action

opening scene   backstory   cliffhanger for a sequel

TWO HOURS

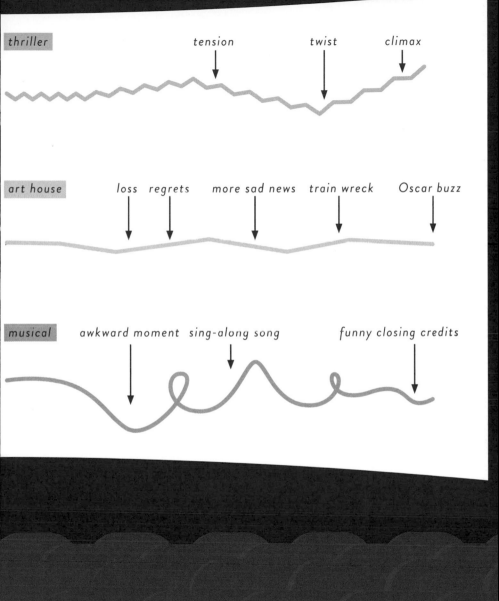

TIME IS MONEY

the older the better

SUNDAY HANGOVER

you booze you snooze

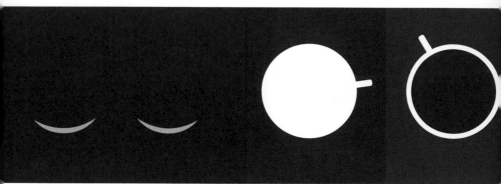

STARTING SLOWLY

lights camera action!

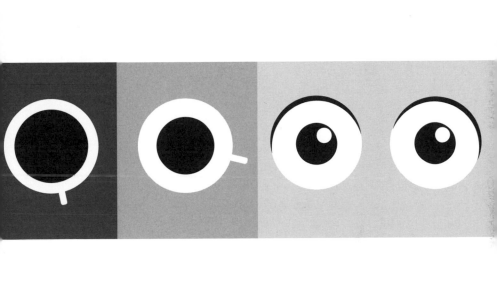

january

may

COUNT DOWN

reset and repeat

september

february

march

april

june

july

august

october

november

december

YEAR ROUND

small talk with your neighbor

TICK TOCK

one day off, never long enough

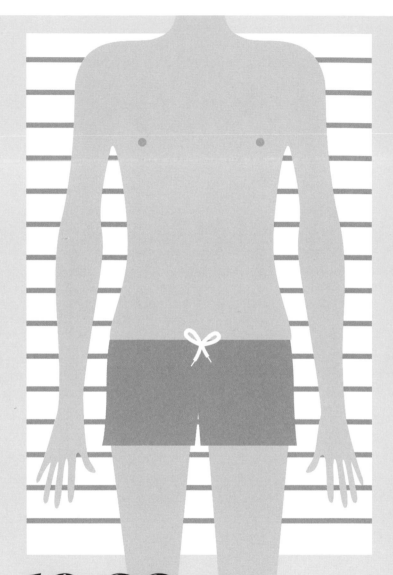

from **10:23**AM *to* **4:07**PM

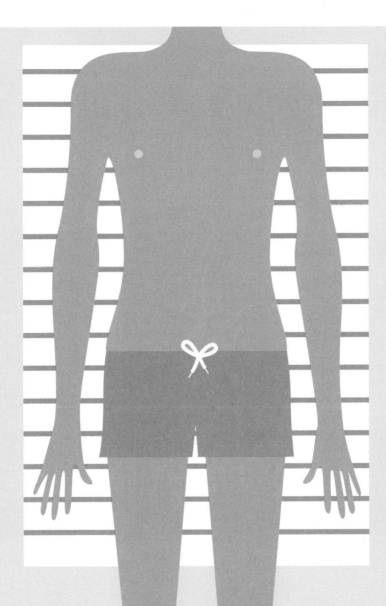

PRESS PAUSE

and unleash your imagination

PAUSE

THROUGH THE AGES

the stories we tell

learning to **LET GO**

BEFORE NIGHT FALLS

let's go

forget something
go back
let's go again

traffic   *change the music*

are we there yet ?   gas refill   final stop   last toll
                                                need to pee ?

home sweet home

SLEEPLESS NIGHT
eyes wide open

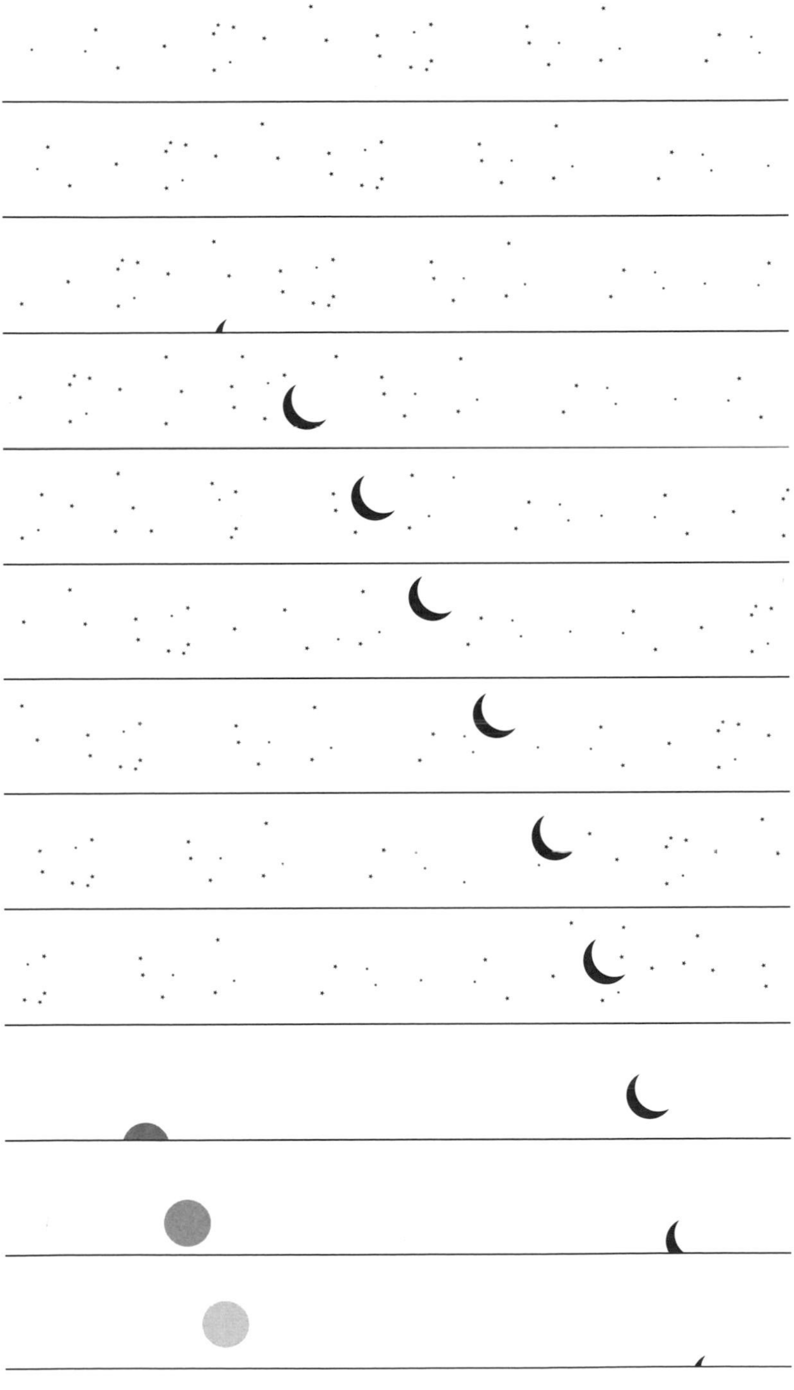

ALL
NIGHT
LONG

there will be blood

zzzzzzzz z z z

BORED *all by yourself*
TO DEATH

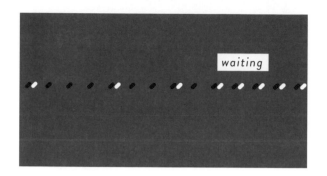

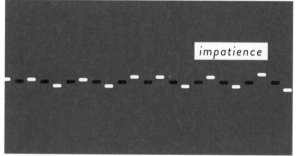

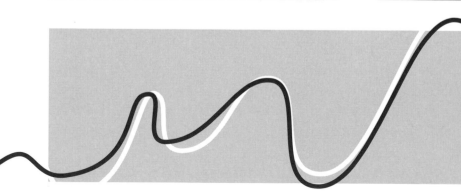

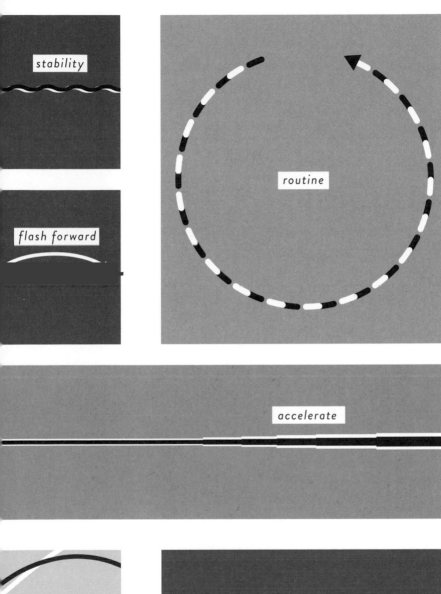

FAST & FURIOUS *dead on time*

PRETTY GOOD DAY

first time in LA

BIG BEN

first time in London

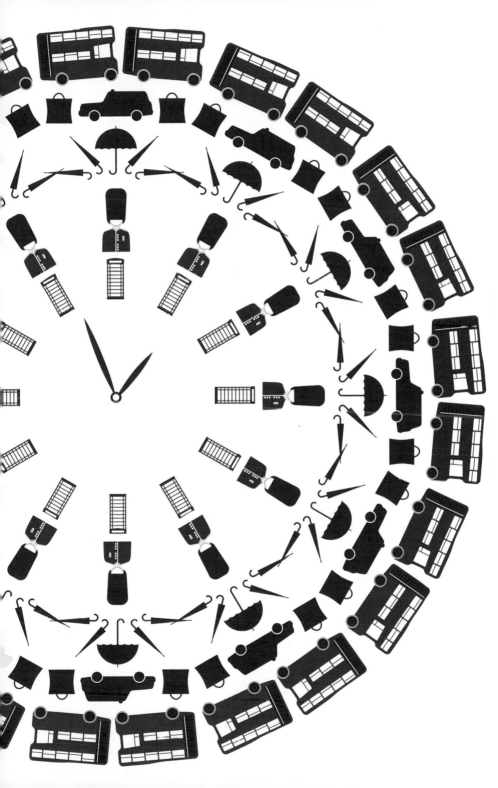

charming bridge

Eiffel tower

selfie

36 HOURS

first time in Paris

fancy
brasserie

Champs-Elysées

Versailles

lost

le Marais

lovely street

SLOWING DOWN

first time in Kyoto

nutmeg

mango

red chilli

curry

cumin

cinnamon

masala

SPICY
MEMORY

first time in Mumbai

ginger

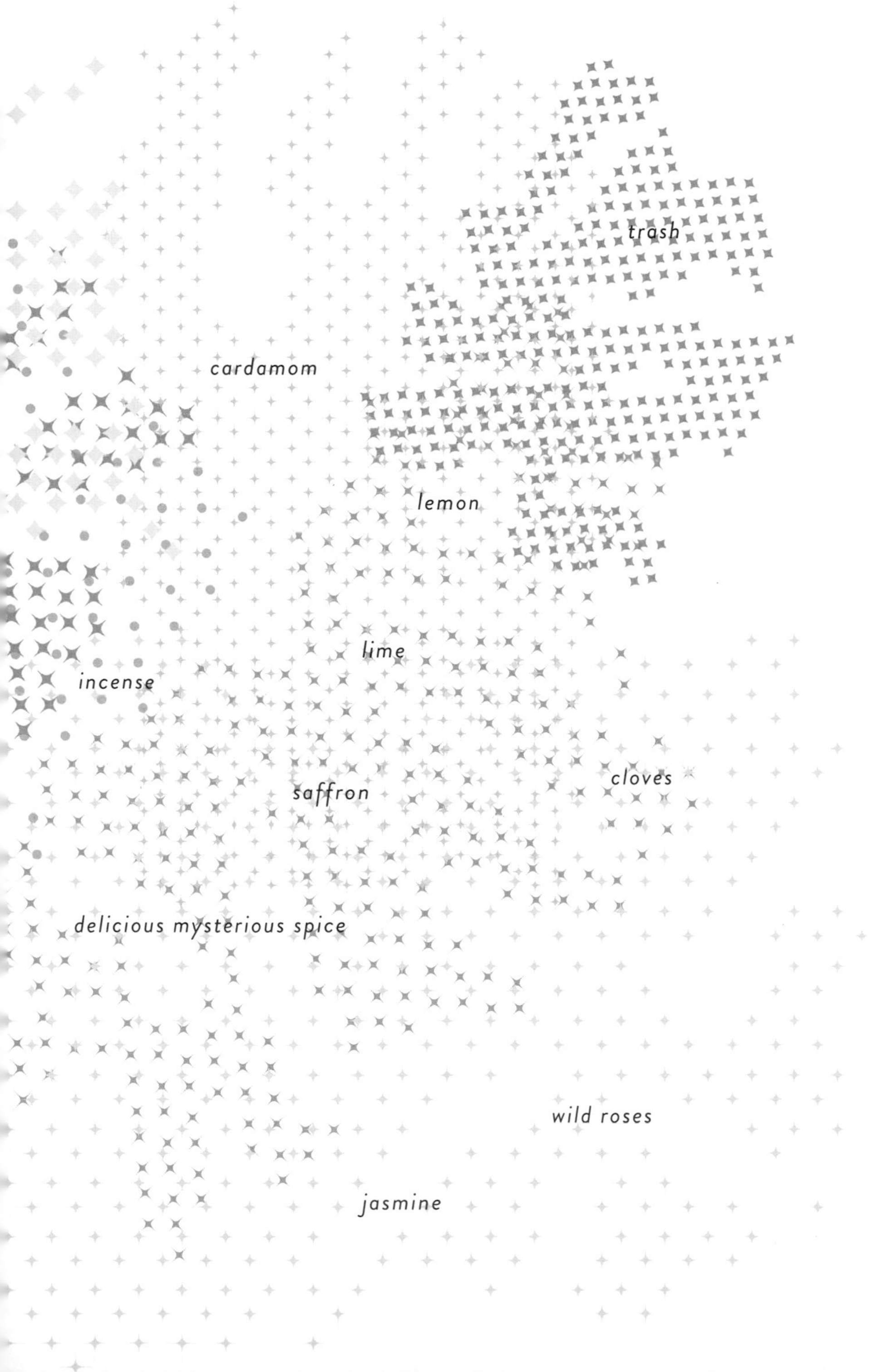

trash

cardamom

lemon

lime

incense

saffron

cloves

delicious mysterious spice

wild roses

jasmine

spring
wet & chilly outside
humid inside

ONE *in New York*
YEAR

winter
cold & dry outside
super hot inside

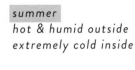

summer
hot & humid outside
extremely cold inside

fall
perfectly mild outside
perfectly mild inside

lost in translation

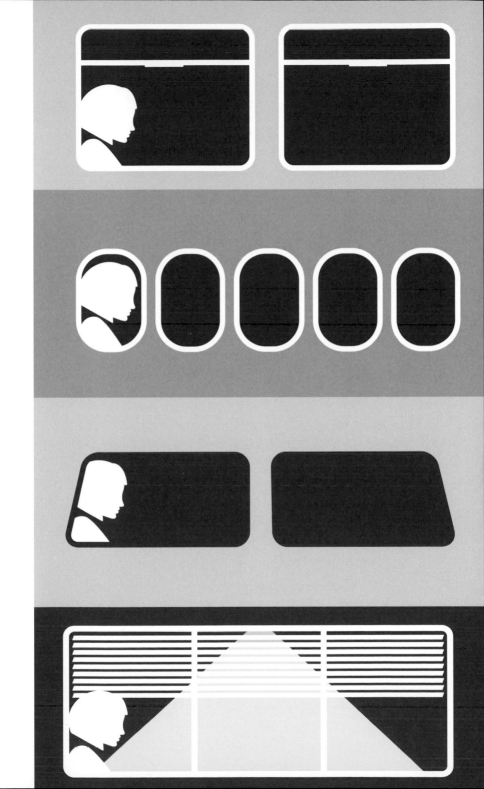

THE MAP OF TIME

Nostalgic Ocean

SORROW

Bitterness Side

Remorse Sea

REGRETS ISLAND

APOLOGYLAND

HUG ISLAND

LOVE ISLAND

PASSION ISLAND

Glory Days Sea

■ LASTWEEK

Blues Sea

YESTERYEAR ■

SHORT-TERM MEMORY

GENUINE ISLAND

JAVA SISTABROTHA

YESTERDAY ■

FLIN
■

Inner Child Sea

NOWORRIES ISLANDS

EL MOMMYDADDY

ROMAN
■

SAN ELDERLY

Bay of Pigs

SHAME ISLAND

Devil's Triangle

LOST ISLAND

MEMORY LAPSE ISLAND

PAST PERFECT ISLAND

SAN DONJUAN

Patience Strait

SMILEYS ISLAND

■ FORGIVE

■ LONGENOUGH

■ AGES AGO

Crazy Canal

■ BEFORE THEFLOOD

Secrets Bay

INTIMATE NATIONAL PARK

← *THE HILLS*

SOUVENIR COUNTRY

■ TEENANGST

■ DECADESAGO

■ BON TEMPS

■ YEARSAGO

Trust Bay

SIN ■
CITY

GETOVERIT ■
CITY

OBLIVION DESERT

Denial Delta

▲ MOUNT SINNER

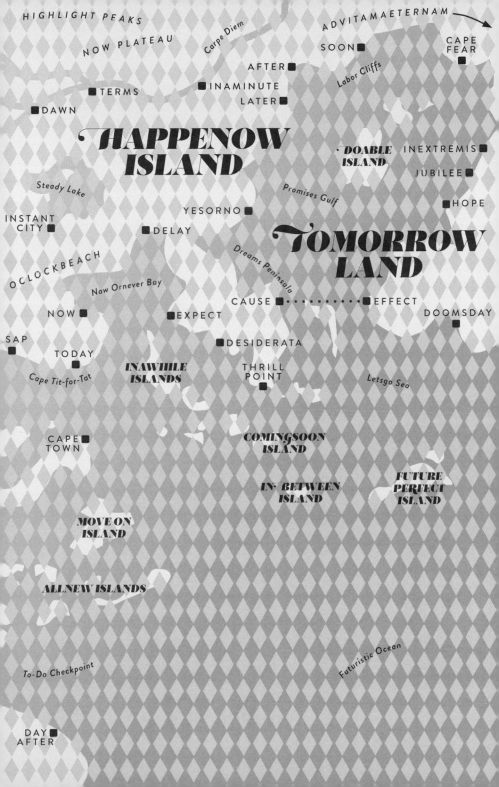

JET LAG

wide awake at 4 AM *sleepy at 4 PM*

HARD DAY'S NIGHT

your space   my space

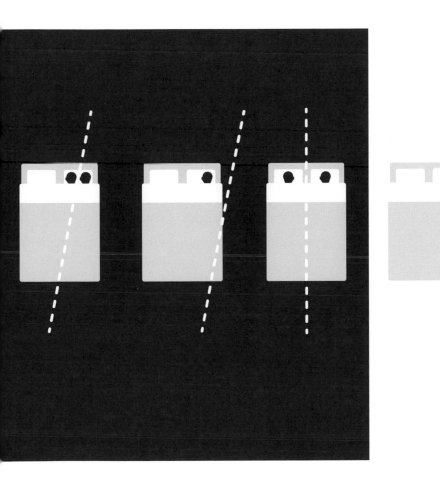

BRAND NEW DAY

sneakers or shoes

t-shirt or button-up

socks or stockings

umbrella or hat

hello
phone, wallet, keys
tie or scarf
v-neck or turtle neck
jeans or skirt
ers or briefs
chic or casual
waking up
radio
breakfast
toilet
shower
sexy or natu
pink or white
blue or black
stripes or colorblock
parka or trench

RUNNING OUT

grooming on the go

EARLY BIRD

no good deed goes unpunished

was it today?

BEST LAID PLANS

they're not coming at all

they don't like me anymore

did they message me?

maybe they're lost

they had an emergency

they're hanging out without me

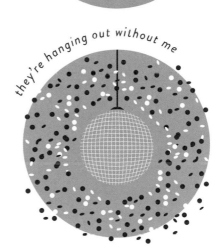

did the worst happen?

about time

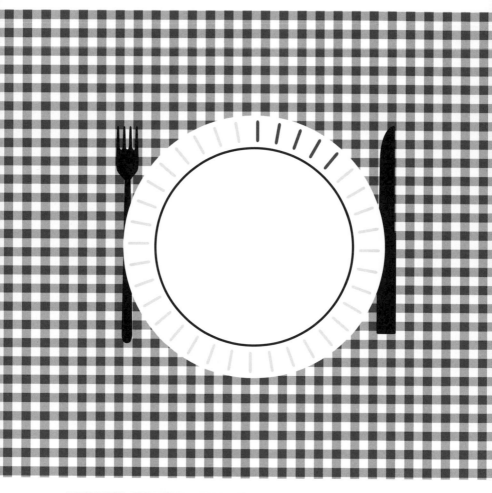

THREE *to cook*
HOURS

TEN *to eat* MINUTES

WHY WAIT

see something, say something

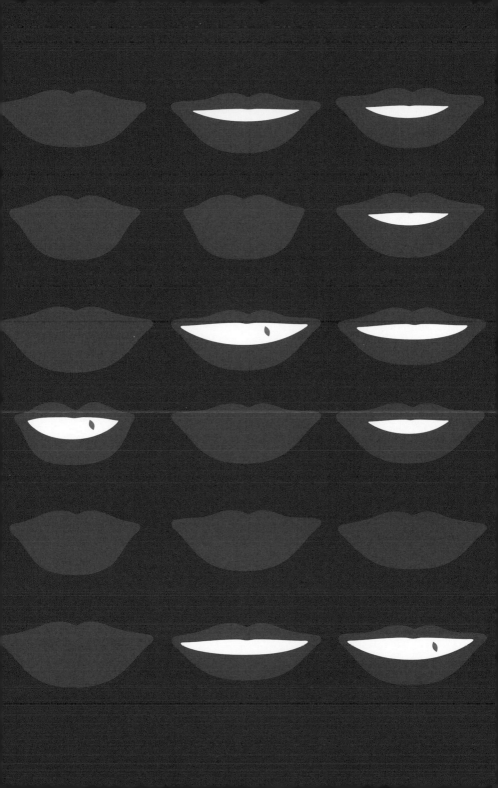

USED TO HATE

turning over a new taste bud

at 15

at 17

at 23

at 25   *at 27*   *at 31*

1977
decorate

1985
trash

QUALITY TIME

conquest of space

2012
bargain-hunt

2014
reinvent

PREDICTABLE BEHAVIOR *doggy-style*

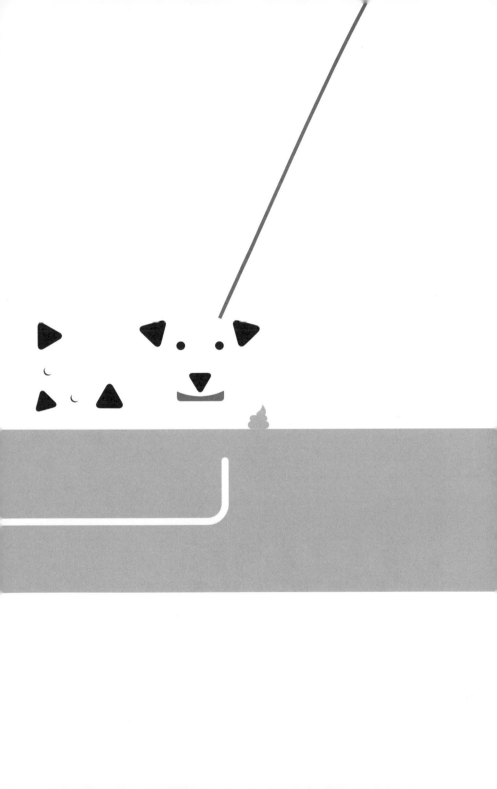

internal time
personal time
people around you
place where you live
international rhythm

LIKE CLOCKWORK

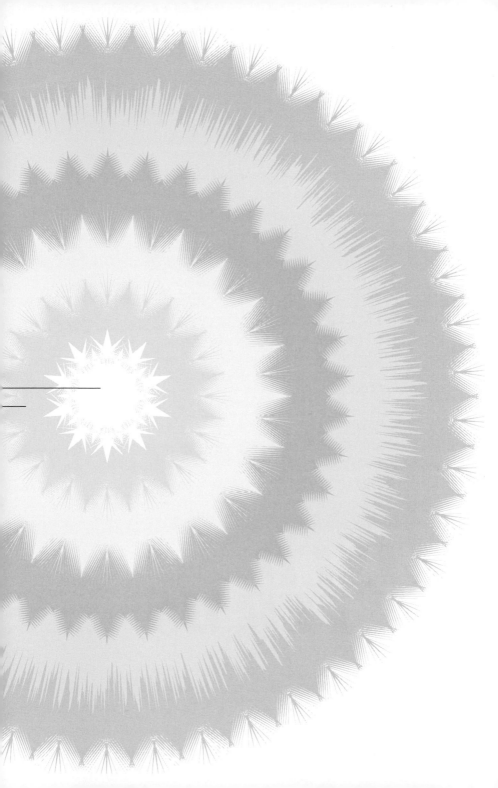

kindergarten

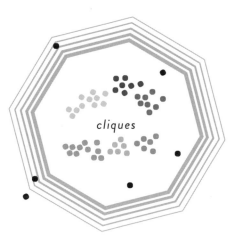

cliques

FIXED *together alone* TERMS

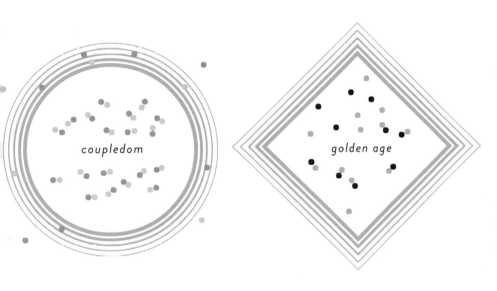

THE
never alone
NEW
NOW

TIME CAPSULE
Sleepy
LAUGH ZONE
Timeoff St.
CHILD HOOD
MOOD HOOD
Principle St.
SUMMER '94
Big Scheme St.
Friendship St.
Mistake Ave.
Frivolity River
OBLIVION
Labor St.
AWKWAR ZONE
Value St.
Choice Place
Vanity Rd.
BLACK OUT ZONE

Fantasy Ave.
GRUMPY ZONE
Party St.
HAPPY SUNSHINE PLACE
Love Blvd.
AMOR
BEST OUND TRACK
Trouble Ave.
Flirty Ave.
HIGH STRESS
Lost Time St.
Conscience Blvd.
Victory Rd.
SCENT HOOD
INNER VOICE
GRANDMA'S KITCHEN
FAMILY DISTRICT
Money St.
Unknown St.
LOST MOMENTS
NOSTALGIA HOOD

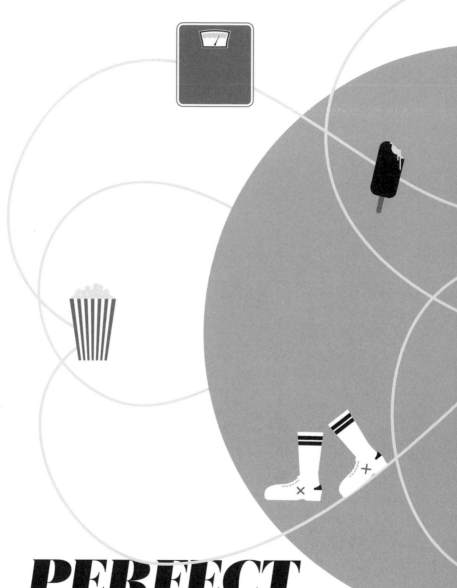

PERFECT TIMING

you are what you eat

① INTERNSHIP

② FIRST JOB

③ FREELANCE

④ NEW JOB

⑤ PROMOTION

STEP *look ahead* BY STEP

GLORY DAY

the road to the corner office

MISSION COMPLETED

hello Florida!

OUT OF SYNCH

is it me or does everyone look so young?

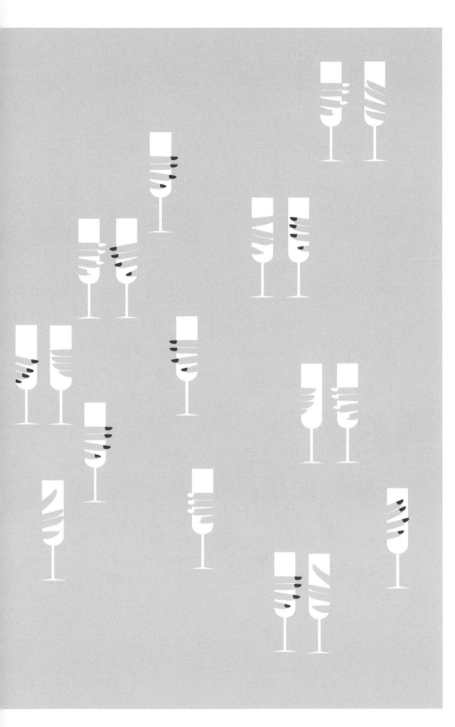

AGE

get by with a little help

WITH GRACE

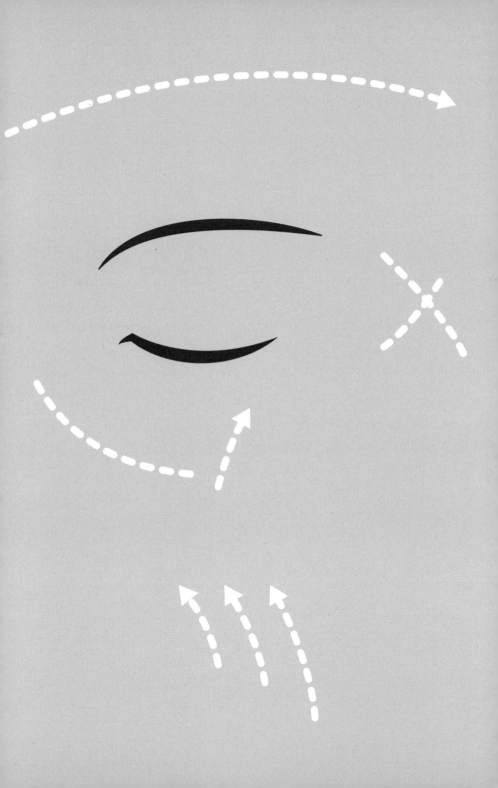

POINT OF NO RETURN

this is not happening

1968

1972

1984

1988

FLASH BACK
just want to have fun

2000

2004

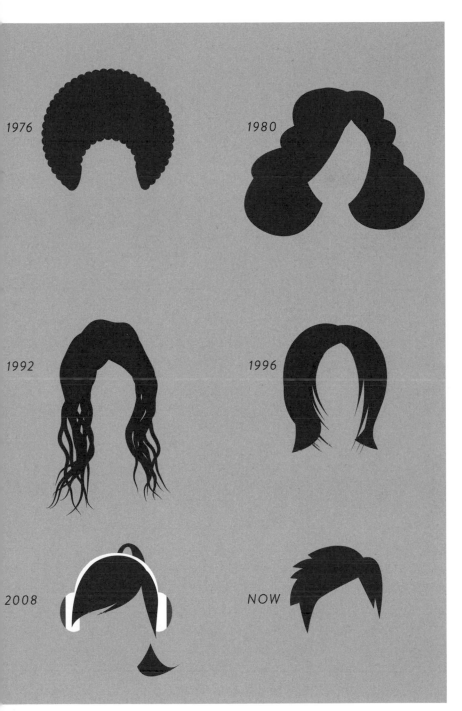

1968

1972

1984

1988

WAY BACK

bad hair days are over

2000

2004

1976

1980

1992

1996

2008

NOW

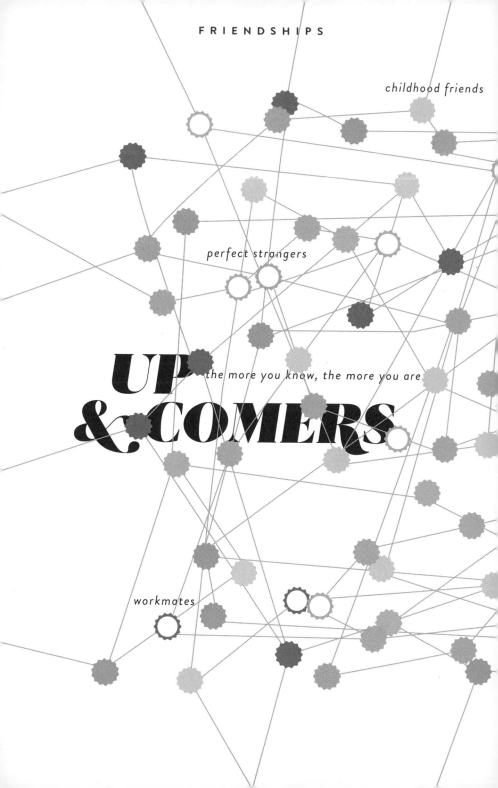

FRIENDSHIPS

childhood friends

perfect strangers

UP
& COMERS

the more you know, the more you are

workmates

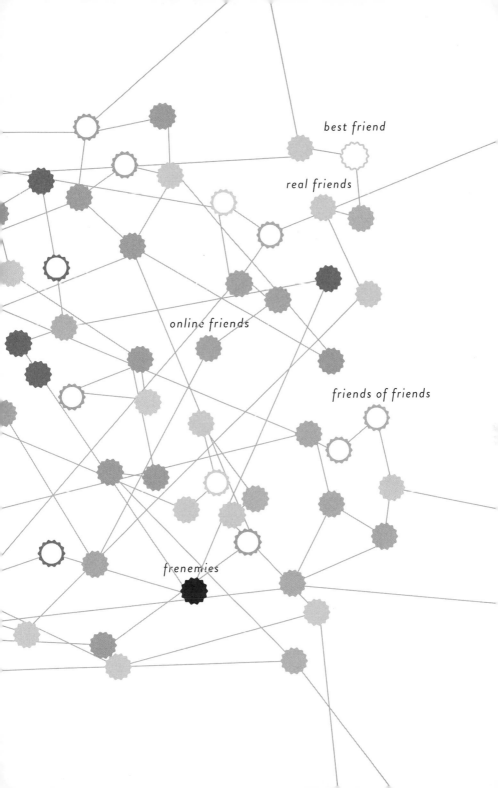

best friend

real friends

online friends

friends of friends

frenemies

LONG TIME NO SEE

see you soon

START SPREADING

the news

Just like the first time, second time around.
After the adventure of *Paris versus New York*, I thank my original editors, Emmanuelle Heurtebize and Laura Tisdel – time flies when you're having fun – Rowan Cope, who arrived just on schedule, the teams at *Stock* in Paris and *Little, Brown* in New York + London. Even allowing for the time difference, the tempo has been perfectly orchestrated by Susanna Lea, with the help of her brilliant team – Mark Kessler, Katrin Hodapp, Laura Mamelok, Kerry Glencorse & co.

THANK YOU

For the happy hours spent exploring the past with Kiraz,
the right words at the right moment from Thiery Teboul Fontana,
the magical weeks with Jim Mersfelder and Sandra Stark,
the precious time Antonin Baudry devoted to his spot-on analysis,
the non-stop caustic humor of Sonia Kalaydjian,
the presence of Marie-Amélie Degail between two of life's milestones,
the perpetual curiosity of Nathalie Rykiel,
the steady support of Sarah and the *colette* crew,
the first three years with the team at *M le magazine du Monde*,
the constant kindness of my family,
all the love and patience that my parents showed
during our quiet mornings together.